HRJC

MAR 2023

EGYPT

BY A. W. BUCKEY

Essential Library

An Imprint of Abdo Publishing
abdobooks.com

ABDOBOOKS.COM
Published by Abdo Publishing, a division of ABDO, PO Box 398166, Minneapolis, Minnesota 55439. Copyright © 2023 by Abdo Consulting Group, Inc. International copyrights reserved in all countries. No part of this book may be reproduced in any form without written permission from the publisher. Essential Library™ is a trademark and logo of Abdo Publishing.

Printed in the United States of America, North Mankato, Minnesota.
102022
012023

 THIS BOOK CONTAINS RECYCLED MATERIALS

Cover Photos: Anton Aleksenko/iStockphoto, pyramid; Shutterstock Images, pattern
Interior Photos: Shutterstock Images, 4–5, 8, 11, 14–15, 23, 42, 60, 80; Matyas Rehak/Shutterstock Images, 13, 50–51; Peter Hermes Furian/Shutterstock Images, 17 (Egypt); Web Tools/Shutterstock Images, 17 (globe); Anton Petrus/Shutterstock Images, 20; Aun Photographer/Shutterstock Images, 21; iStockphoto, 24–25, 30; Dieter Meyrl/iStockphoto, 27; Gideon Ikigai/Shutterstock Images, 31; Agami Photo Agency/Shutterstock Images, 32–33; F. Stuart Westmorland/Science Source, 35; John R. Foster/Science Source, 36–37; DEA/C. Sappa/De Agostini/Getty Images, 39; Patrick Landmann/Science Source, 41; AP Images, 44–45, 46, 47; Bentley Archive/Popperfoto/Getty Images, 49; Gianluigi Guercia/AFP/Getty Images, 55; Liselotte Sabroe/Ritzau Scanpix/AFP/Getty Images, 57; Jean-Claude Deutsch/Paris Match/Getty Images, 58; Hussein Farar/Shutterstock Images, 61; Alex Anton/Shutterstock Images, 62; Tom Bert/Shutterstock Images, 64–65; Richard Drew/AP Images, 68; Fayed El-Geziry/Sputnik/AP Images, 71; Ashraf Shazly/AFP/Getty Images, 73; Khaled Desouki/AFP/Getty Images, 74–75; Anton Aleksenko/iStockphoto, 76–77; Soeren Stache/Picture Alliance/dpa/AP Images, 78; M. Farouk/Shutterstock Images, 81; Tom Carpenter/Shutterstock Images, 83; Ahmed Gomaa/Xinhua News Agency/Getty Images, 85; Andrei Nekrassov/Shutterstock Images, 86–87; Amr Nabil/AP Images, 88–89, 91; Tamer Adel Soliman/Shutterstock Images, 93; Roger Anis/AP Images, 94; Vlad Siaber/Shutterstock Images, 97; Hassan Ammar/AP Images, 98–99; Gil C./Shutterstock Images, 101

Editor: Arnold Ringstad
Series Designer: Maggie Villaume

Library of Congress Control Number: 2022940310

PUBLISHER'S CATALOGING-IN-PUBLICATION DATA
Names: Buckey, A. W., author.
Title: Egypt / by A. W. Buckey
Description: Minneapolis, Minnesota: Abdo Publishing, 2023 | Series: Essential Library of Countries | Includes online resources and index.
Identifiers: ISBN 9781532199394 (lib. bdg.) | ISBN 9781098274597 (ebook)
Subjects: LCSH: Egypt--Juvenile literature. | Africa--Juvenile literature. | Egypt--History--Juvenile literature. | Geography--Juvenile literature.
Classification: DDC 962.0--dc23

CONTENTS

CHAPTER 1
A TOUR OF EGYPT 4

CHAPTER 2
GEOGRAPHY 14

CHAPTER 3
PLANTS AND ANIMALS 24

CHAPTER 4
HISTORY 36

CHAPTER 5
PEOPLE AND CULTURE 50

CHAPTER 6
POLITICS 64

CHAPTER 7
ECONOMICS 74

CHAPTER 8
EGYPT TODAY 88

ESSENTIAL FACTS	100
GLOSSARY	102
ADDITIONAL RESOURCES	104
SOURCE NOTES	106
INDEX	110
ABOUT THE AUTHOR	112

CHAPTER ONE

A TOUR OF EGYPT

Even after two days in Egypt, Remi's eyes are still adjusting to the extremely bright sunshine in Alexandria. It had been a long flight from Boston, Massachusetts. Remi landed in the northern coastal city early in the morning along with her parents and her little brother, Omar. They were greeted by smiling cousins Remi had never met before. They offered Remi a drink of extra-strong Turkish coffee to help her stay awake.

Remi's dad was born in Alexandria, Egypt, but moved to the United States before Remi was born. This is her first time visiting the country she has heard about her whole life. Like most Egyptians, Remi's

Alexandria, one of Egypt's largest cities, is located on the country's Mediterranean coast.

cousins speak Arabic. Remi tries her best to use the phrases she has learned from her dad and grandmother. Remi's cousins are friendly and fashionable. Her cousin Mona shows her how to beat the Egyptian heat with long, flowing clothing. Mona also teaches her how to pin on a hijab, or head scarf. Many Muslim women and girls wear them, and Remi will need one when she visits Egypt's beautiful medieval mosques.

Remi's grandma on her dad's side is Muslim. Her grandma and grandpa on her mom's side are Christian. Remi grew up learning about both faiths. Ever since she can remember, she has been fascinated by the diversity of religious traditions. She plans to major in religious studies in college and maybe become a professor. Remi is eager to see Egypt's religious history and culture up close. She knows it's a majority Muslim country, with a rich tradition of Islamic art and learning. She also knows that Egypt is home to a Christian minority, Coptic Orthodox Egyptians who have practiced their faith since ancient times. And Remi is interested in the religious history of ancient Egypt: the gods, goddesses, and traditions from thousands of years ago. For her parents and brother, this is a big vacation and a family reunion. For Remi, it's also an exciting learning opportunity.

> **THE LIBRARY OF ALEXANDRIA**
>
> If Remi had a time machine, she would have loved to spend a few days at the Great Library of Alexandria. The famous ancient library was established by the ancient Greeks around 300 BCE. By the 200s BCE, the library's goal was to collect every book in the world. Historians estimate that the library may have held as many as 700,000 volumes.[1] In 48 BCE, Roman emperor Julius Caesar set fire to Alexandria, and the library burned down.

THE TRIP TO CAIRO

When it's time to get on the bus to Cairo, a few hours south, Remi hugs Mona and promises to stay in touch. She gets a little sleep on the bus. When she wakes up, she sees the banks of the Nile River, the mighty waterway that runs the entire length of the country. When they arrive in Cairo, Remi is stunned. The city is enormous, with a metropolitan area containing more than 20 million people.[2] The family goes shopping through the Khan el-Khalili, a giant open-air market that has existed since the Middle Ages. Shopkeepers tell her about sales and deals as she sorts through long, beautiful dresses and her mom checks out souvenirs. On the taxi ride back to the hotel, Remi sees three tall stone triangles in the distance. They are the Pyramids of Giza.

The pyramids and the Sphinx, the stone creature with a human head and a lion's body, have been standing in the Sahara Desert for more than 4,500 years.[3] The largest of the three pyramids is about as tall as a 50-story building. Omar thinks the pyramids are cool, but he's distracted by the chance to see a group of camels up close. Remi recalls reading about the beliefs that led to the pyramids' construction. The pharaohs who had these giant pyramids built were buried inside; they believed that they were gods on Earth and that the treasures inside their tombs would prepare them for

> **The Great Pyramid of Giza, originally standing about 480 feet (147 m) high, was the tallest structure in the world from its completion in the 2400s BCE until the construction of England's Lincoln Cathedral in 1311 CE.[4]**

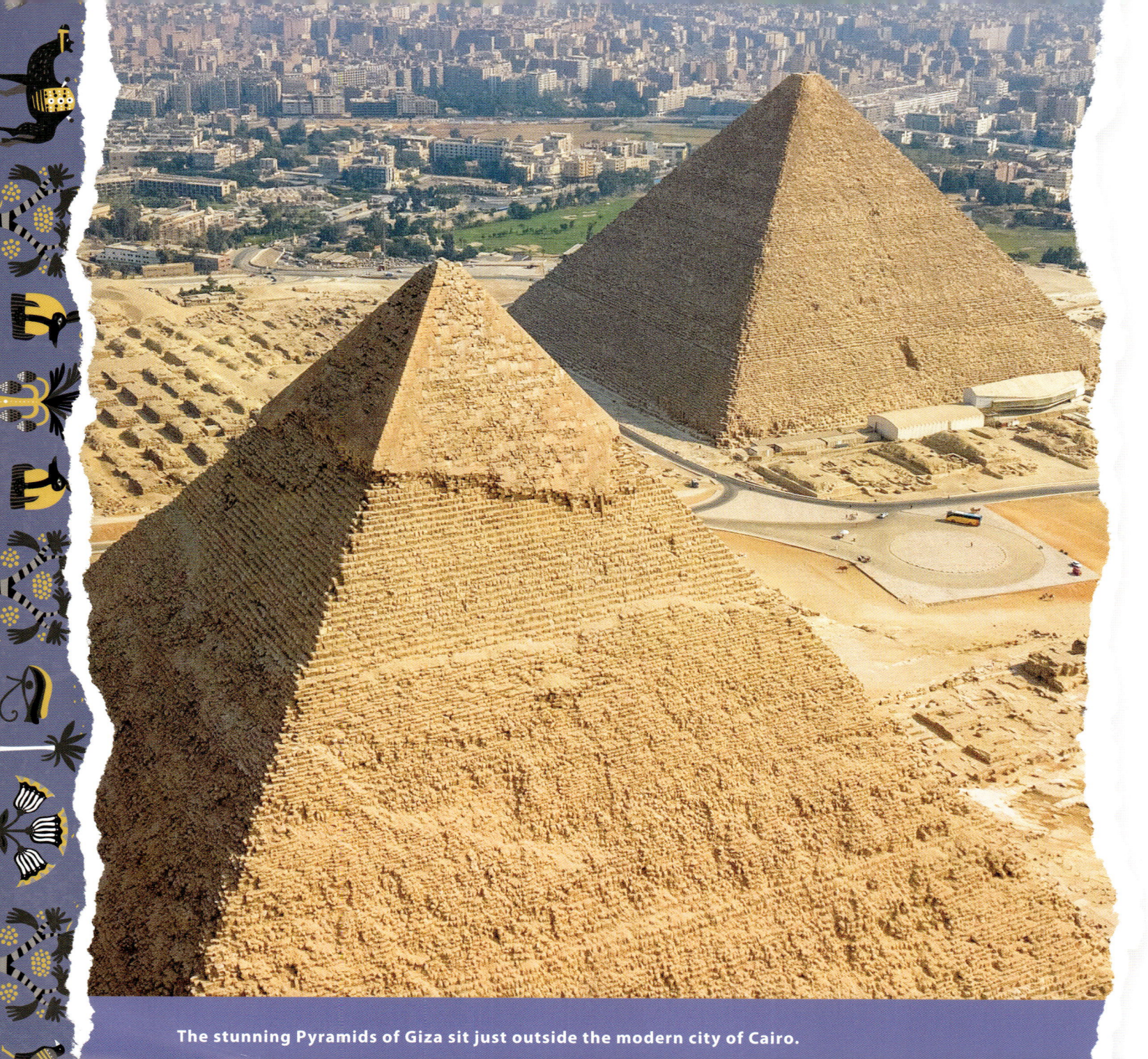
The stunning Pyramids of Giza sit just outside the modern city of Cairo.

> **GIZA**
>
> When the pyramids were built, the pharaohs of Egypt lived in the capital city of Memphis, which is just 15 miles (24 km) south of modern-day Cairo.[5] Khufu, who ordered the construction of the Great Pyramid, chose nearby Giza as his burial site. Giza is now a suburb of Cairo. Its pyramids are a half-hour drive from downtown Cairo and are visible from many places in the city.

a luxurious life after death. Remi takes notes and pictures on her phone, trying to record every detail.

The next day, Remi's family leaves the hotel before breakfast, and they're hungry by the time they get near the Egyptian Museum. Remi's dad leads them to a cart where a man is preparing *koshari*, one of Egypt's most famous foods. Many people make koshari in outdoor carts. The dish has noodles and rice covered in a warm, spicy tomato sauce and topped with lentils and fried onions. It's filling and rich, like a pasta mixed with a curry, with crunch on the top. For the rest of the day, Remi keeps an eye out for other koshari carts. All the walking is making her hungry, and she wants to know if a second bowl will taste as delicious as the first one.

Remi has been to a few museums with ancient Egyptian sections. The one in her home city has a stone slab with hieroglyphic carvings and small statues shaped like people and hippos. But the Egyptian Museum is unlike anything she's ever seen. It is floor after floor of ancient statues, tombs, and colorful papyrus paintings. Each corner of the museum is stuffed with priceless treasures, but Remi knows exactly what she wants to see. Brochure in hand, she leads her mom, dad, and Omar up to the third floor. And there she finds it. A stone slab showing a man wearing the tall

hat of an Egyptian pharaoh. He holds what looks like bunches of flowers up to a shining sun. This is a carving of Akhenaten, the ancient pharaoh who overthrew his country's traditional religion and started his own religion that worshipped only the sun. Remi wonders what the figures in the museum's carvings are thinking and what they believe.

EAST TO SINAI

Leaving Cairo is bittersweet. The city can be noisy and overwhelming, but Remi is going to miss the sights, the smells, and the many, many food carts.

AL-AZHAR MOSQUE

One of the mosques Remi might be most excited to visit is al-Azhar Mosque in Cairo. Al-Azhar Mosque was established in 970 CE when a new dynasty, the Fatimids, conquered northern Egypt. Soon afterward, the mosque also became a center of learning. In fact, Al-Azhar University is one of the oldest universities in the world. The mosque is known for its complex architecture, with additions from many different eras and styles. The university remains a global hub for Islamic learning.

On their fifth day in Egypt, the family takes a bus to Dahab, a small town on the Sinai Peninsula. This is the northeastern part of Egypt, along the Red Sea. The Red Sea separates Africa from Southwest Asia; the Sinai Peninsula links the two continents. Dahab is famous for scuba diving. People come from all over the world to explore the coral reefs along the coast. During the bus ride, Omar can't stop talking about the fish and coral he's hoping to see underwater. He shows Remi pictures of a dugong, an animal in the Red Sea that is similar to a manatee. Omar brags that if there are any around, he'll definitely see them first. Remi laughs. She's excited too.

Dating to the 500s CE, Saint Catherine's Monastery is the world's oldest monastery still in operation.

Remi's family is also planning to go on a hike. They'll travel to Saint Catherine's Monastery, where Christian monks have been living and working for about 1,500 years.[6] The monks who founded Saint Catherine's chose the location for a special reason: it is just beneath Mount Sinai, a very important place for Jews, Muslims, and Christians alike. All three faiths have stories that say Mount Sinai is the place where God gave the prophet Moses, or Musa, the essential laws for humanity to follow. Omar is looking forward to hiking through the desert landscape, and Remi's parents keep saying they need the exercise. Remi can't wait to explore the important religious site.

A COUNTRY OF TRADITION AND CHANGE

People have lived in Egypt for hundreds of thousands of years. Located in northeast Africa, Egypt is home to about 100 million people. It's the third-most populous country in Africa.[7] It is also the most populous Arabic-speaking country.[8] Egypt has a long and rich cultural history. It was the center of an ancient civilization that lasted for thousands of years, becoming part of many different cultures, economies, and international systems.

Egypt is a country of desert and sea, and through it runs the Nile, one of the world's biggest rivers. Today, Egypt is home to rich farmland and huge cities, hundreds of miles of shoreline, mountains and oases, deposits of natural resources, and cutting-edge scientific technology. Recent decades have seen significant political change in Egypt. In 2011, a revolution brought down President Hosni Mubarak, who had ruled Egypt like a dictator for decades. Even after a new constitution and multiple presidents, Egypt continued struggling to find political peace. The country also faces other pressing issues. Global climate change threatens the country's ecosystems and the livelihoods of the people who depend on the seas and the Nile. The people of Egypt work to celebrate their land and heritage while navigating both local and global challenges.

The narrow, busy streets of Cairo are often crowded with shoppers.

CHAPTER **TWO**

GEOGRAPHY

Egypt is located in the northeast corner of Africa. It borders Libya to the west and Sudan to the south. The Sinai Peninsula is located in Egypt's northeast. The peninsula is home to Egypt's tallest mountain, Mount Katrina. The Suez Canal, a 120-mile (193 km) artificial waterway, separates mainland Egypt from the peninsula, which is part of Asia. To the east of the Sinai Peninsula, Egypt shares a border with Israel.

Egypt is the thirty-first largest country in the world.[1] It is almost two and half times the size of California, with a total area of 386,662 square miles (1,001,450 sq km).[2] In addition to its land borders, Egypt borders the Mediterranean Sea to the north and the Red Sea to the east. Egypt is part of the larger

The Nile River makes life possible in a narrow corridor running through Egypt's vast deserts.

> **Mount Katrina, Egypt's highest mountain, is 8,625 feet (2,629 m) tall.**[3]

Mediterranean region, a collection of countries in Europe, Africa, and West Asia that surround the Mediterranean Sea.

Most of Egypt's land lies within the Sahara Desert, the world's largest hot desert. The Sahara stretches over most of North Africa and has a total area of 3.3 million square miles (8.6 million sq km). The Sahara region includes all the other countries in the northernmost part of Africa: Libya, Tunisia, Algeria, Morocco, and the contested territory of Western Sahara. The desert also stretches farther south into Niger, Mauritania, Chad, Mali, and Sudan.

Egypt's location has made it a hub of culture and transportation for thousands of years. It is an African, Asian, Middle Eastern, Saharan, and Mediterranean country. Perhaps the most significant feature of Egypt's geography, however, is the Nile River. The Nile originates in eastern Africa and flows north, with its delta opening into the Mediterranean Sea along Egypt's northern coastline. The Nile River continues to be the center of human activity in Egypt, and it's home to many of its ecosystems.

THE NILE RIVER

The Nile is the longest river in the world. In the south of the country its flow is controlled by the Aswan High Dam, which was completed in 1970. The dam helps manage the annual flooding of

MAP OF EGYPT

KEY:
- 🟥 Capital
- ⚪ City
- 📍 Point of Interest

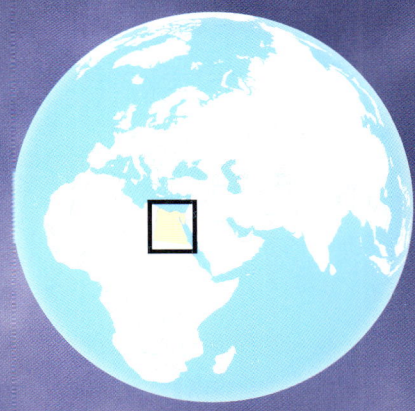

the Nile. The Nile's flooding irrigates the crops that are planted near the river, but it can also be destructive. The dam at Aswan controls the flow of water in the Nile so that it floods Egypt's land in planned amounts. It also provides electricity by generating hydroelectric power. An artificial lake called Lake Nasser is located behind the dam. Lake Nasser helps hold water from the Nile until the dam is ready to release it northward. In the north of Egypt, the Nile River delta empties into the Mediterranean Sea. Because of the direction that the river flows, the ancient people of Egypt thought of the north as Lower Egypt and the south as Upper Egypt. Today, those names are still used for the north and south of the country.

> **NILE FLOODING**
>
> The Nile River follows yearly rhythms of flooding and receding. In Ethiopia, the spring and summer monsoons cause the river to rise. By summer and fall, the rising river waters make their way to Egypt. The resulting floods help water the crops planted along the Nile. For this reason, annual Nile floods have always been important in Egyptian culture. In the 1900s, the construction of the Aswan Dam helped control these floods.

The soil near the Nile is very well suited to growing plants and crops. Silt from the river deposits nutrients into the earth. The river is also a major source of drinking water. It is a means of transportation for people and goods, allowing for both short trips within Egypt and longer journeys to eastern Africa. The Nile helps support the country's fishing industry. The river is so central to life in Egypt that 95 percent of the country's population lives close to its banks.[4] The country's four largest cities, Cairo, Alexandria, Giza, and Port Said, are all along the Nile. Cairo, the largest city and the nation's capital, is located just below the opening of the Nile Delta, and Giza is a few miles south of Cairo. Alexandria and Port Said are on opposite sides of the Nile Delta, bordering the Mediterranean Sea in the north of the country.

THE DESERT AND THE SEA

Egypt's desert land is divided into the Western and Eastern Deserts. These sections of the Sahara lie on either side of the Nile. Because the Nile flows through the eastern part of the country, the Western Desert is much larger than the Eastern Desert. The Western Desert makes up two-thirds of Egypt's land, and the Eastern Desert makes up one-fourth. The Western Desert is home to several oases, areas in the desert with fresh water and plant life. Some of these oases, such as the Siwa Oasis, have been homes to people for thousands of years. The Eastern Desert is sandy, irrigated by channels called wadis, and home to a chain of small mountains near the Red Sea. Most of Egypt's oil fields, as well as natural resources such as manganese and gold, are found in the Eastern Desert. The land of the Sinai is mostly dry and

> ### THE GEOLOGY OF THE SAHARA DESERT
> The Sahara isn't only flat, sand-covered terrain. Its land includes rocky areas, mountains, areas of shifting sands called ergs or sand seas, and low basins called depressions. The lowest part of the Sahara, the Qattara Depression, is located in Egypt. The depression drops 436 feet (133 m) below sea level.[5] Water in the Sahara is found in aquifers, which are rock basins that hold groundwater, and in streams and wadis.

The White Desert in central Egypt features distinctive limestone rock formations.

desertlike as well, but the peninsula is not considered part of the Sahara Desert. Southern Sinai is Egypt's most mountainous region and home to all its tallest peaks.

Egypt has 1,522 miles (2,450 km) of coastline. For millennia, Egyptians have lived, traded, and fished near the sea. Ocean shipping is a big business, with 90 percent of the world's goods transported over sea routes, and Egypt plays an important role in this industry.[6] Egypt has 15 commercial ports, or places where ships can dock to load and unload goods. The country is also home to 29 specialized ports, which serve a single purpose such as hosting cruise ships or oil shipments.[7] Egypt's biggest ports are near Alexandria, Port Said, and the two openings of the Suez Canal. Many smaller ports are clustered around the Red Sea. On the eastern shore of Egypt, people live in small fishing villages and make their living from the ocean. The Sinai Peninsula and the Red Sea are also home to long stretches of coral reefs.

THE SUEZ CANAL

The Suez Canal was finished in 1869. It uses water from several lakes in the Sinai Peninsula to create a waterway from the Mediterranean Sea to the Red Sea. Before the canal was built, it was very difficult for boats to travel between the Atlantic and Indian Oceans. The Suez Canal created a shortcut that ships could use to transport people and goods. Today, it is one of the most-used routes for transport ships in the word.

EGYPT'S CLIMATE

As part of the greater Sahara Desert region, Egypt's climate is generally hot and dry. The country gets very little rain, which is another reason the Nile's waters and floods are so crucial to human life. Temperatures can vary greatly across different ecosystems. The Sahara, for example, is legendary for its heat. In the summer, temperatures in southern Egypt can regularly reach 109 degrees Fahrenheit (43°C).[8] However, desert temperatures often drop dramatically at night. This is because deserts are covered in sand and rock, which radiate energy from the sun, and because the desert air is too dry to retain heat. On desert nights, with dry air and no sunlight to reflect on the sand, temperatures can drop to freezing. Areas near the ocean tend to have more moderate temperatures year-round.

Egypt, like many places on Earth, has seen its average temperatures rise in recent decades. Human contributions to climate change, such as increases in carbon emissions, have led to hotter temperatures across the globe. In addition, sea levels have also risen worldwide. The melting of ice in the Arctic and Antarctic, as well as the expansion of warmer water, have led to higher sea levels along Egypt's northern and eastern coasts. This rise in sea levels can threaten settlements along the shoreline. Higher sea levels mean that more of the Nile River delta is covered by the ocean, changing its ecosystems. Higher temperatures can also lead to the drying out of the basins that supply the Nile with its water. This threat to the river's water supply comes at a time when Egypt's population and water needs are growing. If the Nile is unable to provide enough water for Egypt's crops, the consequences for the country's people and environment could be severe.

Areas on the coast typically have more comfortable temperatures than Egypt's desert regions, with an average annual temperature of around 70 degrees Fahrenheit (21°C).

CHAPTER THREE

PLANTS AND ANIMALS

Egypt's plant and animal life is as diverse and varied as the country's geography. Many of the Nile's plants and animals have captured the attention of human beings for millennia. The blue lotus flower that grows on the Nile is an ancient symbol of rebirth. The flower emerges at the top of the water during the day and sinks back down underwater at night. Today, the blue lotus is the national flower of Egypt. The papyrus plant is an aquatic plant that once grew along the entire length of the Egyptian Nile. It has tall stalks that can grow up to 15 feet (4.6 m) high, and its top fans out like a triangle. The ancient Egyptians

The papyrus plant has been an important part of Egyptian culture for thousands of years.

figured out how to make paper from the fiber inside the plant. In fact, the word *paper* comes from the word *papyrus*.

Today, papyrus plants no longer grow in large numbers along the Nile's banks, though they are cultivated by Egyptian farmers. However, the banks of the Nile host a great variety of other plant life, both wild and human-grown. Palm trees grow along the Nile, and so do acacia trees—small, shrub-like trees with a fanned shape. Reeds and grasses, as well as bamboo, also grow in and along the Nile's waters. The date palm, frequently mentioned in the Bible and the Muslim holy book called the Qur'an, is found near the delta of the Nile River. The Nile also irrigates the crops and plants that are most widely cultivated in Egypt, including sugarcane, sugar beets, wheat, and corn.

The Nile River is home to more than 800 species of fish, but not all of them make their way to the lower part of the river in Egypt.[1] Lake Nasser is a major site for the Egyptian fishing industry. About 90 percent of the fish caught there are tilapia, a type of fish often used in cooking.[2] Other Egyptian fish include several species of catfish, as well as the Nile perch, which can grow to the weight of a

> **PAPYRUS MAKING**
>
> The ancient Egyptians had many uses for the papyrus plant, turning it into cloth and sails. Egyptians were also the first people to make paper out of papyrus. Ancient Egyptians first started using papyrus as a writing material around 3000 BCE. They combined sheets of fiber and rolled them into scrolls, wrapping them around wooden sticks. The ancient Greeks and Romans borrowed the technique from the Egyptians and used papyrus in their papermaking as well.

More than 3,000 fishing boats are licensed to operate on Lake Nasser.

human, and the marbled or leopard lungfish. The marbled lungfish is a unique animal. It has the ability to breathe air, and it can walk on fins that resemble small legs. It is a large fish that can grow to more than four feet (120 cm) in length.[3] In dry periods, marbled lungfish bury themselves in cocoons and create a small air passage through which they can breathe. Several species of reptile also live in the Nile River in Egypt, including water snakes and the Egyptian banded cobra.

Above and along the Nile, many species of birds make their homes. Egrets, geese, ospreys, hawks, and herons all live near the Nile River. In ancient times, Egyptians especially revered the ibis, a black and white bird that hunts in shallow waters. Today, the national bird of Egypt is the steppe eagle, a brown eagle that scavenges for its food.

Crocodiles and hippopotamuses used to live all along the banks of the Egyptian Nile. Over time, their habitats have decreased in size. Today, crocodiles in Egypt are mostly limited to the southern part of the country, near Lake Nasser, and hippopotamuses are no longer found in Egypt.

PLANTS AND ANIMALS OF THE EGYPTIAN DESERT

There is little plant life throughout most of the Egyptian Sahara, and the animals that live in this

CROCODILE HUNTING

It's unknown how many crocodiles live in Egypt, but experts agree that the crocodile population has greatly decreased in recent years. One reason for the decrease is a rise in poaching, or illegal hunting. People who hunt crocodiles can sell their body parts in markets throughout Africa and western Asia.

ecosystem must adapt to barren conditions. The Western Desert is an especially challenging place to live, and some parts of it have no plants at all. Grasses and hardy plants called succulents, which store water, grow in the Egyptian desert, and there are trees in the Eastern Desert. For example, the tamarisk tree is a shrublike tree that can survive on small amounts of water. There is very little forested land in Egypt.

The largest wild mammal in the Egyptian Sahara is the aoudad, a type of sheep. Other mammals include the jerboa, a long-legged jumping mouse, and the Nubian ibex, a goat that is skilled at mountain climbing. The Egyptian desert is home to the fennec fox and the African wildcat. The house cat was domesticated from this wildcat species.

Only about 0.05 percent of Egypt's land is covered by forest.[5]

Vipers, cobras, and rattlesnakes live in the Egyptian desert. The Egyptian cobra, a hooded species, can grow to 6.5 feet (2 m) long.[4] The horned viper, also called a sidewinder, is known for its S-shaped movement across the hot desert sands. It does this to avoid touching the sunbaked ground with too much of its body.

Scorpions are arachnids related to spiders. The scorpions that live in Egypt have venom that can be deadly to humans. The fat-tailed scorpion is especially dangerous. These scorpions can find their way into human homes after Nile floods or heavy rains. The country's insects include types that are found in many places on the planet, such as ants, butterflies, and mosquitoes. The most

The fennec fox has multiple adaptations to help it survive in desert environments, including large ears to dissipate heat and fur-covered feet to protect its footpads from the hot sand.

famous Egyptian insect is the scarab, a beetle that rolls balls of animal dung across the desert. These dung balls provide food and a place for the beetles to lay their eggs.

> **THE SCARAB IN ANCIENT EGYPT**
>
> The Egyptian scarab's Latin name is *Scarabaeus sacer*, or "sacred scarab." When the ancient Egyptians saw the beetle rolling balls of dung across the desert, they were reminded of the way the sun travels across the sky. They saw the scarab as a symbol of the sun god, Ra, and of rebirth. As a result, people wore scarab jewelry for protection and decoration.

Domesticated animals are an important part of daily life in Egypt. The dromedary, or one-humped camel, is a desert-dwelling animal known for its ability to survive a long time without water. It was first domesticated in West Asia between 3000 and 2000 BCE. Today, camels are mostly important for the tourism and entertainment industries. Guides offer camel rides to international travelers, and camel racing is a traditional sport in the country. Donkeys are also used as transport animals, and buffalo, cows, sheep, and goats are other important domestic animals.

PLANTS AND ANIMALS OF THE MEDITERRANEAN AND RED SEAS

The Mediterranean Sea and the Red Sea are connected in modern times by the Suez Canal. They are both habitats for marine mammals such as whales and dolphins. Sea turtles and ocean fish also swim in these waters.

The shores of the Red Sea in Egypt are lined with coral reefs. These reefs are formed when corals, small sea animals that gather in groups, secrete a rocklike substance called calcium carbonate. Young corals grow on the hard secretions formed by the older ones, and the resulting reef structures provide shelter for fish and other wildlife. The coral reefs of the Red Sea are home to colorful fish such as the spotted snake eel, the lionfish, and the Red Sea clown fish, as well as predators such as the great barracuda. Whales, sharks, and dolphins swim in the Red Sea, and the manatee-like dugong has habitats there too.

EGYPT'S CHANGING ECOLOGY

Just as climate change threatens Egypt's temperature balance and the Nile's waters, it also poses a threat to Egypt's plants and wildlife. In addition, human activity, such as construction, scuba diving, fishing, and shipping, can damage delicate ecosystems. In 2020, 110 Egyptian animals were listed as threatened or endangered. For example, hunting and poaching have greatly decreased the numbers of Egyptian tortoises, which are native to the Nile Delta.

In 2021, the International Union for Conservation of Nature (IUCN) identified 11 Egyptian plant species as "globally threatened."[6]

The dugong eats seagrasses along the floor of the Red Sea.

The Egyptian government and international nonprofits are working to protect Egypt's wild plants and animals from human and environmental threats. For example, the Ministry of Environment's National Biodiversity Strategy is trying to increase the seeding of threatened plants as part of its 2015–2030 Action Plan.

Research shows that the Red Sea's coral reefs are receding. In 2021, the Egyptian government launched a campaign to preserve the Red Sea's environment. The government is partnering with the tourism companies that profit from the sea's reefs to find sustainable, eco-friendly ways for people to interact with the ecosystem.

The reefs of the Red Sea are filled with a wide variety of ocean life, including about 300 types of coral and more than 1,000 fish species.

CHAPTER FOUR

HISTORY

Traces of ancient tent poles indicate that people may have lived in Egypt as early as 700,000 years ago. These people would have lived a nomadic lifestyle, moving from place to place while hunting and fishing. Over tens of thousands of years, these people learned how to grow wild plants like wheat in certain areas. Eventually, they domesticated crops and stayed in one place to farm them. Archaeological evidence shows that by 9000 BCE, a group of people was farming and fishing by a lake near Giza. These people developed their own styles of pottery and their own ways of storing supplies such as grain. Over time, this lake culture and several others built more complicated homes. They buried their dead

Historians have pieced together the story of Egypt's early history using a wealth of archaeological evidence, including the hieroglyphs ancient Egyptians left behind.

in rituals and traded with each other. By 3100 BCE, they had begun to write in symbols called hieroglyphs. This is when the history of ancient Egypt begins.

ANCIENT EGYPT AND NUBIA

The ancient Egyptian culture developed and grew over the course of thousands of years. The early Egyptian pharaohs, the godlike kings who ruled over large sections of the Nile, lived more than 5,000 years ago. Even the ancient Greeks saw those rulers as ancient. Cleopatra, the Greek ruler who was queen of Egypt from 51 to 30 BCE, was alive closer to the modern day than she was to the construction of the pyramids.

Historians recognize four especially significant periods in this long and complex cultural history. In the Old Kingdom, from about 2575 to 2130 BCE, the great pyramids of Giza were constructed. During the Middle Kingdom, from 1938 to about 1630 BCE, a civil war that had divided Egypt was resolved, and Upper and Lower Egypt were united. In the New Kingdom, from 1539 to 1075 BCE, Queen Hatshepsut ruled as the first female pharaoh. After about 1000 BCE, Egypt was invaded and briefly ruled by neighbors and enemies, such as

HATSHEPSUT

Hatshepsut was the ruler of Egypt from 1479 to 1458 BCE. While she was not the first female ruler of Egypt, she was the first to occupy the traditionally male role of pharaoh. As pharaoh, Hatshepsut was often depicted in statue form as a male. This may have been a way of demonstrating her power in a time when king was considered a higher position than queen. Hatshepsut was a successful ruler who promoted peace and trade.

the Libyans. The ancient Persian Empire, based in what is now Iran, conquered Egypt in 525 BCE. In 332 BCE, ancient Egypt's independence came to an end when the ancient Greek conqueror Alexander the Great took over the country. Alexander named a city, Alexandria, after himself and established a Greek dynasty in the country.

Ancient Egyptians remain famous for their art, architecture, inventions, and daring construction projects. Ancient Egyptians were among the earliest world cultures to invent writing. They used a hieroglyphic, or picture-based, system to write down messages. Some of the hieroglyphs represented whole ideas or words, while others were like letters in an alphabet. The ancient Egyptians also invented paper, plows for farming, door locks, and toothpaste. However, the ancient Egyptian culture may be best known for its religion. The people of ancient Egypt believed in many gods and a life after death. Important

Ancient Nubia created an alphabetic writing system called Meroitic. It is not well understood today.

people were buried with objects meant to help them navigate death and live well forever.

The land of what is now Egypt was also occupied by Nubians in ancient times. Ancient Nubia stretched from southern Egypt into northern Sudan and a small piece of present-day Libya. Some of the first state governments in the world originated in Nubia. The Nubian culture was similar to Egypt's in many ways. For example, Nubians also built pyramids. The histories of Nubia and Egypt were intertwined, with each culture conquering parts of the other's territories over the course of ancient history.

> **ALEXANDRIA**
>
> Alexander the Great established the city of Alexandria in 332 BCE and made it Egypt's capital. Its position on the Mediterranean Sea made it easy for Greek rulers to access. The Ptolemaic, or Greek, dynasty was based in Alexandria, the home of Cleopatra. Alexandria was known as a great academic and scientific city. It was home to a lighthouse called Pharos, one of the Seven Wonders of the Ancient World. Alexandria also became a Christian religious center after the religion emerged in the first century CE.

ARAB AND MUSLIM EGYPT

The Prophet Muhammad lived from about 570 to 632 CE in the Arabian Peninsula, across from the Red Sea and Egypt's Sinai Peninsula. He founded the religion of Islam in the early 600s and began campaigns to conquer nearby land. After his death, his followers continued expanding Muslim territory. By 639 they had reached Egypt, which was a largely Christian country at the time. Over the next few hundred years, Egyptians converted to Islam, and the language of the land

Mummies, tombs, and elaborate burial rituals are among the most famous legacies of ancient Egypt, and they have taught scholars a great deal about the culture's history.

switched from Egyptian to Arabic. Egypt came under the control of several large Arab Islamic empires during this time. One empire, the Fatimids, were Isma'ili Muslims, followers of a small sect of the Shia branch of the Islamic faith. In 969, the Fatimids conquered the Arab city of al-Fustat, renaming it Al-Qāhirah, or Cairo. Fatimid influence did not last, and Egyptian Muslims continued to follow Sunni Islam, the other major branch of the Islamic faith. Cairo became Egypt's capital and a major center of Islamic wealth and learning.

THE ROSETTA STONE

Over time, Egyptian speakers began to write in the Greek alphabet. The meaning of ancient Egyptian hieroglyphics was lost for many years. In 1799, a French man in Egypt discovered a stone with writing in multiple languages. The same message was written in Egyptian hieroglyphics, another Egyptian script, and ancient Greek. This stone became the key to decoding hieroglyphics. Scholars who read Greek were able to translate the ancient Egyptian symbols.

THE MAMLUK SULTANATE AND OTTOMAN EMPIRE

In 1250, Egypt was conquered again, this time by the Mamluk Sultanate. The word *Mamluk* is Arabic for "slave." During this time, there was a large international slave trade that stretched across Europe, Africa, and West Asia. It was common for Muslim rulers to enslave boys from places in West Asia and Eastern Europe and train them to become soldiers. Eventually, these enslaved soldiers revolted and started their own empire. Until the 1500s, the majority Arab country was ruled by a small Turkish minority of Mamluk origin. The Mamluks were known for their love of art and architecture, and Cairo flourished as an artistic city.

In the 1500s, the Ottomans conquered Egypt. The Ottoman Empire, based in Turkey, was a massive Islamic empire that once stretched across West Asia and into Europe, the Arab peninsula, and North Africa. Large sections of the empire were ruled by viceroys who held a lot of independent power. The French dictator Napoléon Bonaparte overtook Egypt in 1798 and briefly ruled it, but Ottoman viceroys were still present in the country. By the end of the 1800s, the British Empire was effectively ruling Egypt. However, Ottoman viceroys still led the country in name and mounted some successful revolts against British control.

FATIMID AND AYYUBID EGYPT

The Fatimids renamed their settlement next to al-Fustat "Al-Qāhirah," or "the Victorious," when their caliph, or leader, came to live there in the 970s. The Fatimids ruled an empire covering North Africa, southern Europe, and West Asia with ambitions to take over the Muslim world. Eventually, the famous warrior Saladin was the empire's downfall. Saladin, born in what is now Iraq, was famous for capturing Jerusalem from European crusaders' control. He went on to found the Ayyubid dynasty in Egypt in 1173.

EGYPT IN THE 1900S

During World War I (1914–1918), Egyptians were required to fight on behalf of the British colonizers. About one million Egyptian soldiers fought in the war, and they were treated very poorly.[1] Mistreatment of the Egyptian soldiers spurred unrest and the 1919 Revolution. After the revolution, Egypt technically became independent from the United Kingdom. However, in practice, the United Kingdom retained a lot of control over the country.

After Egypt's independence in 1922, a king named Fu'ād began ruling the country. In 1936, he died, and his teenage son, Farouk, took the throne. Egyptian soldiers were again required to fight for the United Kingdom in World War II (1939–1945). However, few Egyptians supported the British side in the war. In fact, some members of the Egyptian army collaborated with German forces to try to get the British out of the country.

King Farouk was disliked by both the British and the Egyptians. He was seen as weak and vain, with little real power. In 1952, a group of soldiers led by Gamal Abdel Nasser overthrew the king. Nasser became president of Egypt.

Unlike Farouk, Nasser was a powerful and charismatic leader. He was a hero to many, and his political ideas became known as Nasserism. Nasser believed that Egypt and other Arab countries should develop their economies and empower their people. Nasserists, inspired by the Soviet Union in Eastern Europe and Asia, wanted a socialist government that would distribute the wealth from the nation's

During World War II, major battles between the British and the Germans took place in Egypt's northern deserts.

Egyptian troops took control of the Suez Canal from the British in 1956.

resources to all Egyptians. Nasser nationalized many Egyptian businesses and industries, making them government-owned rather than private property.

Nasser's most famous economic move was the nationalization of the Suez Canal. The canal earns money from the ships that pay to pass through it. Before the 1952 revolution, European business interests received almost all the revenue from the canal. In 1956, Nasser brought the canal under Egyptian control, rerouting all of that money to Egyptians. Nasser also oversaw the construction of the Aswan High Dam, which would help control the Nile's flow and provide affordable hydroelectric power. However, empowering the Egyptian government also meant empowering Nasser himself. Nasser was a hero to many, but he ran unopposed in national elections, allowing only one political party to exist in the country. He heavily censored Egyptian media and sent his enemies to concentration camps.

In 1970, Nasser died of a heart attack. He was widely mourned in Egypt. His funeral was attended by as many as six million people, and non-Egyptian Arabs also mourned him as a hero.[2] His successor was Vice President Anwar Sadat. Sadat undid some of Nasser's work on

Anwar Sadat took power after Nasser's death in 1970.

In 2021, the Suez Canal earned Egypt a total of $6.3 billion in revenue.[4]

economic nationalization. He went to war with Israel; in 1973, his military succeeded in taking the Sinai Peninsula back from Israeli control. Five years later, in 1978, Sadat shared the Nobel Peace Prize with Israeli leader Menachem Begin for his work negotiating peace. Sadat grew more authoritarian over time, jailing more than 1,500 people who protested his policies.[3] In 1981, he was assassinated by a member of an extremist group. His successor was his vice president, Hosni Mubarak, a war hero because of his command of the air force in the 1973 war against Israel. Mubarak ran the country for the next several decades.

MINI BIO

GAMAL ABDEL NASSER

Gamal Abdel Nasser was one of Egypt's most influential leaders. He was born in 1918 near Alexandria. Despite coming from a poor family, Nasser was able to get an education. He joined the government as a postal worker and soon became interested in national politics. Nasser opposed British colonial rule of Egypt in the 1930s and was injured at protests. Eventually, Nasser joined the Egyptian military and dethroned Egypt's king. Installing himself as president, Nasser led a one-party, socialist-influenced Egypt. He is famous for his national economic projects, including the construction of the Aswan High Dam and the nationalization of the Suez Canal. He fought wars with Israel in 1956 and 1967. Egypt's defeat in the 1967 Six-Day War dented Nasser's reputation as a strong leader. Nasser is remembered both as a visionary for a more independent Egypt and as a president with unlimited authority and a repressive government.

Nasser survived an assassination attempt in late 1954.

CHAPTER FIVE

PEOPLE AND CULTURE

In 2022, slightly more than 107 million people lived in Egypt. The country's largest population center is Cairo. The greater Cairo area is home to almost 21 million people, or about one-fifth of Egypt's population.[1]

The official religion of Egypt is Sunni Islam, the most widespread of Islam's two main branches. Islam, Christianity, and Judaism are the religions that are officially legal to practice in the country. About 90 percent of Egyptians are Muslim, and about 10 percent are Christian. Members of other faith traditions, including the Baha'i, make up a small minority.[2]

Cairo's bustling city center features a mix of historic sites and modern Egyptian culture.

Historically, Egypt has been home to Jewish communities. For example, the famous medieval Jewish scholar Maimonides came to live in Egypt in 1168 CE. He was attracted by the religious tolerance of the country and wanted a place where he could openly practice his faith. In 1937, during the Egyptian monarchy, about 65,000 Jews lived in Egypt. Just after World War II, the number was around 85,000.[3] However, when Egypt's neighbor, the state of Israel, was founded, about a quarter of Egyptian Jews left the country, with many settling in the new nation.[4] While Israel and Egypt have had relatively friendly relations in recent years, the countries have been at war four times. During the first years of Nasser's presidency, some Egyptian Jews supported British control of the Suez Canal. Nasser seized Jewish-owned businesses, and he pressured or forced thousands of Jews to leave the country. Today, the Jewish Egyptian population is tiny, at only about 100 people.[5]

Egypt's population rose from 69 million to more than 102 million between 2000 and 2020.[8]

The vast majority of Egyptians, more than 99 percent, identify their ethnicity as Egyptian.[6] However, there are some small immigrant groups in Egypt, including the country's Armenian community and the non-Arab Beja people who herd cattle and camels in the desert. Egyptians tend to be young. About 51.6 percent of Egyptians are age 24 or younger, and just 4.4 percent of the people in the country are older than age 65.[7]

ARABIC AND OTHER LANGUAGES

Arabic is the official language of Egypt and is the most widely spoken language. Arabic is a very old language. Today it is spoken across a wide geographical area that spans from Mauritania in West Africa to the Arabian peninsula in West Asia. The Qur'an is written in Arabic, and the form of Arabic used in the Qur'an has been memorized, quoted, and studied by Muslims ever since it was first written down in about 650 CE. As a result, the written form of Arabic has changed relatively little over time, while the spoken forms of Arabic vary much more widely.

A dialect of Arabic called Modern Standard Arabic, or *Fusha*, is like a spoken form of written Arabic and is used in formal contexts like news broadcasts. Most Egyptians, however, use an Egyptian Arabic dialect to communicate in everyday life. The best-known Egyptian Arabic dialect, Cairene Egyptian Arabic, is known for its unique pronunciation of certain sounds. For example, Egyptians tend to pronounce Arabic's soft *j* sound as a hard *g* sound. The pronunciation of the first name of former Egyptian president Gamal Abdel Nasser reflects this change. Other Arabic speakers might pronounce his name as "Jamal," but the English spelling reflects the Egyptian pronunciation.

Some words and phrases in Egyptian Arabic give evidence of the country's multicultural history. For example, Egyptians use the phrase *"tuta tuta"* to end a story told to young children. This phrase comes from the ancient Egyptian word *twt*, which meant "finished." The word *shantah*, meaning "bag," originally came from Turkish. Other Egyptian dialects include Bedouin Arabic and Upper Egyptian, or Sa'idi, Arabic.

A minority of Egyptians speak languages other than Arabic. Some Nubian people in the south of the country speak Eastern Sudanic languages. The people of the Beja nomadic group speak their own languages. Egyptian children learn English as a second language in school.

Before the Arab conquest of Egypt in the 600s and for some time afterward, Coptic was the most spoken language in the country. The Coptic language is descended from ancient Egyptian. In fact, the name *Copt* comes from the same ancient Greek origin as the name *Egypt*. Today, the Coptic language is used in Coptic Orthodox religious services, but it is not spoken in daily life.

ARTS, CULTURE, AND ENTERTAINMENT IN EGYPT

Egypt is a center of culture and entertainment for the Arab world. Although many independent media outlets work in Egypt, the government has the power to censor TV, radio, and print journalism in the country. Nevertheless, Cairo is an international hub for Arabic language TV and movie production. Egyptian Media Production City is a large film and TV production facility near Cairo, and it is often called the Middle East's Hollywood. The center includes sets and sound stages similar to the ones in Hollywood, as well as 80 TV and radio studios.[9] Most Arabic language cable channels are connected in some way to Production City.

Egyptian TV and radio are so influential in the Arabic-speaking world that Arabic speakers in many different countries can easily understand the Cairo Egyptian Arabic dialect in addition to their native one. In Egypt, TV plays a big role in the month of Ramadan. During Ramadan, Muslims do not eat or drink during the day. At sunset, it's common to break the fast with a meal called an

A crew films an Egyptian soap opera at Egyptian Media Production City.

iftar. Muslims often use iftars and the nights of Ramadan as a time to gather and celebrate with family and friends. Since the invention of TV, special TV shows scheduled for Ramadan nights have become popular parts of the evening festivities. These shows may be multilayered soap operas or dramas that tackle complex historical stories and themes. One popular Egyptian Ramadan series is called *El-Ekhteyar*, or *The Choice*. The show follows the stories of members of the Egyptian Armed Forces.

Egypt is also a vital part of the Arabic literary tradition. The most famous modern Egyptian novelist, Naguib Mahfouz, was the first Egyptian and first Arab to win the Nobel Prize in Literature. More recently, Alaa al-Aswany has become one of the Arab world's biggest literary stars. Al-Aswany was born in 1957, the son of a writer who used a traditional form called *maqāmah*, short stories written in rhyme. After being educated in France and the United States, al-Aswany began a career as a dentist while pursuing writing in his spare time. His 2002 novel, *The Yacoubian Building*, became an international best seller and was later adapted as a movie and television series. The novel discusses

NAGUIB MAHFOUZ

Naguib Mahfouz was a novelist and screenwriter who won the Nobel Prize in Literature in 1988. Mahfouz was born in Cairo in 1911. Like his father, he became a government employee. Mahfouz spent a long career in government service, even after gaining great fame for his novels. His work examined Egyptian history and society, tackling controversial topics such as religion and governmental change. He eventually wrote more than 30 novels, and more than 30 movies were made from his books and stories.[10]

the inhabitants of a single building as a way of highlighting a variety of issues that ordinary Egyptians face. Al-Aswany's following novel, *Chicago*, offered similar critiques of the United States. Al-Aswany has been outspoken about his criticisms of the Egyptian government in his art and his public life. In 2019, the Egyptian military sued al-Aswany for insulting the president after he published an anti-government opinion article in a German newspaper.

Egypt has an ancient and rich musical tradition. The ancient Egyptians made music with drums, wind instruments such as flutes, and stringed instruments such as harps. Just as the Coptic language evolved from ancient Egyptian, many scholars believe Coptic Christian chants have their roots in ancient Egyptian music. And in the 1900s, popular singers and entertainers helped revive the country's tradition of classical Arabic music and singing. The most

Alaa al-Aswany's novel *Chicago* is named for the city where he attended dental school.

MINI BIO

UMM KULTHŪM

Umm Kulthūm was born with the name Fatima in 1904. She grew up in a musical family that did not have much money. When she was young, she dressed as a boy in order to perform, since women and girls were not encouraged to sing publicly. She had a low, powerful voice that needed no microphone, and she had a unique approach to classical Arabic music. She was known for the length of her performances. She could spend more than an hour singing a single song, repeating and improvising phrases. Umm Kulthūm married twice to men and may have had romantic relationships with women. When she died in 1975, her funeral was attended by millions of Egyptians, and she was mourned nationwide. In 2001, the Egyptian government opened a museum in her honor. She is sometimes called "the fourth pyramid," a reference to her iconic status in Egypt.[11]

> **Umm Kulthūm has been called *Il Sit*, meaning "The Lady."**

famous of these singers was Umm Kulthūm. Her epic hours-long performances of Arabic songs made her an international sensation. She sang classical Arabic songs in her own unique style and became a symbol of Egyptian pride. Entertainers like Umm Kulthūm also helped pave the way for Arabic language pop music. In the early 2000s, Egypt also developed its own hip-hop tradition. Artists such as Marwan Moussa and Wegz have reached the top of the Egyptian charts with their rap music.

The most popular sport in Egypt is soccer. Egypt's national men's soccer team ranked thirty-second in the world as of 2022, and its women's soccer team came in ninety-fifth.[12] The Egyptian Premier League was founded in 1948 to allow professional teams from many different regions of the country to play together. In 2022, 18 professional teams played in the league.[13] Egyptian soccer games get front-page news coverage, and the biggest soccer stadium in Egypt, Borg Al-Arab near Alexandria, seats 86,000 people.[14] Exceptional soccer players such as Mohamed Salah have become stars in Egypt.

Egypt is also home to some of the world's best squash players. Squash, or squash tennis, is a two-person racquet game played indoors on a small court. Players stand on either side of a divided court, volleying a small rubber ball against a wall and into each other's sections. The game requires speed and agility. In April 2022, the top three women's squash players in the world were all Egyptian. In addition, Egyptian men held the second, third, and fourth spots in global player rankings. Egyptian players believe that the tight-knit squash community and the country's reputation for excellence help young players dream big and progress quickly in the sport. "We had a lot of champions growing up," Ali Farag, the number two men's player, explained to a journalist. "Those players were always generous. . . . We're all concentrated in Cairo or Alexandria, so we can play against each other."[15] The country is so dominant in squash that it has changed the way the game is played. Egyptian-style squash favors surprise attacks and powerful shots over traditional strategies like trying to tire out an opponent.

EGYPTIAN FOOD AND DRINK

Egyptian cuisine shares many recipes and ingredients common to Arabic, North African, and Mediterranean cultures. For example, Egypt's most common bread, *aish baladi*, is like a pita. Hummus, tahini, and meat kebabs are Egyptian staples. Fava beans are a major ingredient in Egyptian cooking. A fava bean stew called *ful* is a common breakfast food, and the Egyptian version of falafel, *ta'ameya*, is made with fava beans rather than the chickpeas used in a typical falafel. While Egyptian cities, like American ones, are populated by pigeons, in Egypt

MOHAMED SALAH

Mohamed Salah, also known as Mo Salah, is an Egyptian soccer player. Salah was born in 1992 in Basyoun, Egypt. He began playing for a professional Egyptian club in 2010, and he was later recruited to play soccer in Europe. Since 2017, he has played as a forward for Liverpool FC, a team in the United Kingdom's Premiere League. In 2017, he set a record for the number of goals scored by a Premier League player. Although Salah's main career is in the United Kingdom, he also plays for Egypt's national team in international and World Cup matches.

Koshari is a popular street food in Egyptian cities. The dish, which originated in India, was brought to Egypt in the 1800s by the British.

pigeon meat is roasted and eaten as a delicacy. Fish such as sardines and tilapia are plentiful in Egypt and make up a large part of the Egyptian diet. Koshari is one of the most distinctive Egyptian dishes. Egypt's most popular desert is called *umm Ali*. It is similar to bread pudding and contains coconuts and raisins.

Tea and coffee are both popular drinks in Egypt and are served indoors and outdoors all day. Egyptians also enjoy drinking *karkadeh*, an herbal tea made from hibiscus leaves. Islam prohibits drinking alcohol, and alcohol use is not an open part of everyday life in Egypt. However, it is legal to buy alcohol in the country, and some breweries have operated in the country in recent years. Tobacco use is very common in Egypt, however. About 20 percent of Egyptians use tobacco, and cigarettes are the most common form.[16] Rates of death from tobacco-related illnesses are high in the country.

URBAN AND RURAL LIFESTYLES

Egyptian people live within cities, near oases, along the coastline, and in the desert. A little less than half of Egyptians are city dwellers.

Cairo Tower, a famous structure in the capital, is among the tallest buildings in Africa.

Cairo has the largest metropolitan area. The second-largest metropolitan area is Alexandria and its surroundings, with a population of about 5.5 million.[17]

Rural Egyptians mostly live in small villages or larger towns clustered around the Nile River. These villages are typically surrounded by farmland, and about a quarter of Egyptians work in agriculture.[18] People who live in rural areas in Egypt are significantly more likely to be poor than urban Egyptians. Upper, or Southern, Egypt is also a poorer area than Lower Egypt. A 2014 study by the Brookings Institution found that 83 percent of the poorest people in Egypt live in Upper Egypt.[19]

Of the 5 percent of Egyptians who do not live near the Nile, many live in oceanside settlements, in the Sinai Peninsula, or in towns such as Mut, which borders an oasis in the Sahara in western Egypt. A small minority of Egyptians live nomadic or seminomadic lifestyles, moving from place to place and caring for animals. This lifestyle is also called pastoralism. Some of these nomadic people are Arabic-speaking Bedouins, who mostly live in the Sinai Peninsula.

> **BEDOUIN LIFE**
>
> The word *Bedouin* is Arabic for "desert dweller." It describes a lifestyle, not an ethnicity. Bedouins identify with Arabic culture, but they typically do not live in cities or towns. Bedouins herd animals and often work as guides in the tourist industry. Some Bedouins live in tents that can be packed up and moved from place to place.

CHAPTER SIX

POLITICS

Hosni Mubarak was first elected president of Egypt in 1981. Almost 30 years later, at the beginning of 2011, he was still president of Egypt. At first, Mubarak's time as president was characterized by strong relationships with other Middle Eastern countries. He was also seen as a reformer who undid some of the repression of Sadat's presidency, freeing political opponents from prison. Mubarak was reelected four times, but each election was considered suspicious. Few voters showed up to vote, and there were signs that the voting numbers were faked or tampered with. Over time, Mubarak was seen as overly harsh in his response to political opponents. He especially targeted Islamist activists, or people who believe that governments should use Islamic laws

Thousands of Egyptians crowded the streets during the protests against Hosni Mubarak in early 2011.

to construct their political and legal systems. Mubarak was also blamed for rising poverty and inequality in the country. Many suspected that he planned to make his son Gamal president after he stepped down instead of holding free elections.

In 2011, opposition to Mubarak's presidency reached a high point. Egyptian protesters were influenced by the wave of Arab Spring protests that began in 2010 in Tunisia and spread rapidly with the help of social media. Across the Arab world, activists connected over platforms such as Facebook and Twitter to organize protests. The protests in Egypt began in December 2010. By early 2011, thousands of protesters, congregating in Cairo's Tahrir Square and elsewhere, were calling for Mubarak to step down. Mubarak retaliated at first, leading to hundreds of casualties in the country. Finally, in February 2011, he stepped down as president, and the Egyptian Armed Forces took control of the country. His successor, Mohamed Morsi, took power in 2012 after a nationwide election in which multiple candidates competed for the presidency. Morsi was a longtime member of the Muslim Brotherhood, a political group that has historically been banned in Egypt.

As president, Morsi got rid of a constitutional decree that limited the power of the president, and

TAHRIR SQUARE

Tahrir Square is a public square near the center of Cairo. The word *tahrir* means "liberation" in Arabic; the square was renamed Tahrir following the 1952 revolution. The square is located near several important government buildings, and it is a popular place for protests and demonstrations. During the Arab Spring protests against Mubarak, the square was packed with thousands of people.

he drafted a constitution without input from many members of Egypt's Parliament. In December 2012, Morsi declared martial law in order to retain his power. In 2013, the head of the Egyptian Armed Forces, Abdel Fattah el-Sisi, removed Morsi from the presidency. In the process, more than 1,000 people were killed in clashes between pro-Morsi protesters and el-Sisi's forces.[1] After Judge Adly Mansour briefly held the position of interim president, el-Sisi won the presidential election in 2014.

Turnout in the 2014 presidential election was low, at about 46 percent.[4]

El-Sisi was reelected in 2018. As in previous presidential elections, it was widely suspected that el-Sisi owed his presidential win to corruption. He gained 97 percent of the vote in the election, an enormous margin of victory.[2] At the time, Egypt's constitution allowed presidents to lead the country for a maximum of two four-year terms. In 2019, el-Sisi's Parliament approved a new constitutional amendment that would allow him to run for another two terms, potentially remaining president until 2030.

El-Sisi has been widely criticized for arresting protesters and members of opposition parties. In 2019, for example, his government arrested more than 2,300 anti-government protesters, some of them children and teens.[3] El-Sisi is also known for his censorship of various forms of media, including print, TV, radio, and internet journalism. El-Sisi has used military force to arrest, imprison, or torture political opponents.

El-Sisi addressed the United Nations General Assembly in 2019, discussing international conflicts, terrorism, and other issues.

THE ARAB REPUBLIC OF EGYPT

Egypt's official full name is the Arab Republic of Egypt, reflecting the pan-Arabist ideas of the Nasser era. A republic is a government that holds free elections and is led by a president. Although Egypt has both a president and a prime minister, the president is the head of the executive branch of government.

Egypt's laws are made by a bicameral Parliament, meaning that the lawmaking body has two parts. Egypt has a Senate with 300 seats and a House of Representatives with 596 seats.[5] The election and appointment process for House and Senate seats is complex. For example, one-third of the Senate's 300 seats are appointed by the president rather than elected. In the House of Representatives, most members are chosen with a simple election process. Another portion of the members are chosen in a separate system that sets quotas for representation for women, young people, Christians, and other groups.

PAN-ARABISM

Pan-Arabism is a belief that Arabic-speaking countries share a core common culture. Therefore, pan-Arabists argue, Arab people and countries should unite to pursue shared political and economic goals. Pan-Arabism became most popular in the mid-1900s, when many Arab countries became independent from European colonial rule. Another event around this time, the discovery of oil in the region, quickly enriched many Arab countries. Pan-Arabists such as Nasser advocated for Arab countries to unite and share resources. In this way, pan-Arabists said, the Arab world as a whole would be richer and more powerful.

VOTING, PROTESTS, AND POLITICAL MEDIA

Egypt has experienced a great deal of political turmoil since 2010. Elections are widely regarded as corrupt and unfair, and many sources of political news are censored by the government. As a result, the political scene in Egypt is complex and difficult to navigate. New political parties come and go, and many struggle to find a foothold in Egyptian politics. There are also political groups in

Egypt that do not have the status of official parties. The largest and most influential is the Muslim Brotherhood, a political group that advocates for a government based on Islamic principles. The Muslim Brotherhood has been officially outlawed many times throughout the country's history. Morsi came from a Muslim Brotherhood background, and the party was banned again after he was removed from office. However, some political parties in Egypt are led by Muslim Brotherhood members who promote the organization's goals.

Other political parties are more secular, or interested in nonreligious government. Additionally, the Egyptian Armed Forces have a great deal of influence in political matters. In the 2018 Parliamentary elections, four parties gained the majority of available Parliament seats. Two of these parties were secular. They were the Wafd, a liberal nationalist party, and the Free Egyptians Party, a secular liberal party. The other two, the Nation's Future Party and Homeland's Defenders, were new parties that were close to the military. One Islamist party, the al-Nour party, gained some seats.

Because of the turmoil and corruption of Egyptian elections, many young Egyptians are

THE MUSLIM BROTHERHOOD

The Muslim Brotherhood was founded in 1928 by Egyptian Islamist and political leader Hassan al-Banna. Al-Banna called for an Islam-based government to correct the damage of European colonialism in Egypt. The Muslim Brotherhood has been and continues to be influential in Egyptian politics. It first organized anti-government protests during World War II. Many Muslim Brotherhood members participated in anti-Mubarak protests in 2011.

skeptical of voting. The 2018 presidential election had only a 40 percent turnout, with many young Egyptians boycotting what they saw as an unfair process.[6] In 2018, college student Yousef Shandawely explained that he lost faith in Egypt's elections after the candidate he supported, along with four other candidates, dropped out of the race. "I will not participate in the elections," Shandawely told *USA Today*, "and don't be surprised if, after a while, [people protest.]"[7]

COUNTERTERRORISM, DISSENT, AND FOREIGN RELATIONS

Terrorism is a genuine threat in Egypt. One branch of the terrorist group Daesh, the militant group also known as the Islamic State in Iraq and the Levant (ISIL), is based in the Sinai Peninsula. The international community also monitors two groups in Egypt that are affiliated

The results of the 2018 election were seen as suspiciously one-sided.

with the terrorist organization al-Qaeda. Terrorist groups have targeted the country's Coptic Christian minority.

A 2021 report by the International Commission of Jurists found that el-Sisi's administration uses laws against terrorist activity to silence and persecute human rights activists. For example, the court pointed out that el-Sisi's government has placed lawyers and human rights defenders on terrorist lists. The country's counterterrorism laws allow the government to designate citizens as terrorists without any evidence of wrongdoing. Such laws also allow the government to jail these people without giving them the opportunity to have a trial.

El-Sisi has a strong connection to Egypt's large and powerful military, the Egyptian Armed Forces. Military service is mandatory for Egyptian men between 18 and 30 years old. The Egyptian military has historically received a great deal of aid from the US military. Much of this aid helps Egypt purchase weapons. For example, most fighter jets in the Egyptian Air Force's arsenal are F-16 Fighting Falcons purchased from the United States.

With its status as the largest Arab country and one of Africa's largest nations, Egypt often plays a large role in international diplomacy. The country is a member of the United Nations, the African Union, the Arab League, the World Bank, and many other international organizations. As a member of the Arab League and the home of its headquarters, Egypt has sought peaceful solutions to disputes in the Arab world and has worked to further the interests of the league's members. It has also worked toward unity for Africa's nations.

Egyptian soldiers participated in a joint training drill with Sudan in the desert northwest of the Sudanese capital, Khartoum, in 2021.

CHAPTER SEVEN

ECONOMICS

Egypt has the second-largest economy in Africa and the twentieth-largest in the world. The country is rich in natural resources and has many thriving industries. However, income inequality is high, and almost one-third of Egyptians live in poverty.[1] Despite its economic challenges, Egypt was one of the few countries in the world to experience economic growth in the first few years of the 2020s.

The Egyptian currency is the Egyptian pound. One pound is divided into 100 piastres. In 2022, the exchange rate with US currency was approximately 18.5 Egyptian pounds to one US dollar.[2] Banknotes are available in denominations ranging from 25 piastres up to 200 pounds, and they feature images of historical Egyptian architecture.

Massive construction projects illustrated the strength of Egypt's economy in the early 2020s.

HOW THE EGYPTIAN ECONOMY WORKS

Countries structure their economies differently according to their political philosophies, cultural preferences, and national interests.

> Egypt's gross domestic product (GDP), the total value of its goods and services, was about $365 billion in 2020.[3]

One important economic distinction is the one between capitalist and socialist economies. In capitalist economies, also called free-market economies, the government does not do much to regulate business. In socialist economies, the government controls many key resources. For example, a socialist government might nationalize all electric companies. Electric company employees would be paid by the government. The government could then choose to charge people less money for their electric bills than a private company might. The Egyptian economy is somewhere between a capitalist and a socialist one, with some unique features of its own. Its economic approach is sometimes called state capitalism.

The Aswan High Dam is a key component of Egypt's economy. Its hydroelectric generators produce a significant amount of the country's electricity.

Today, Egypt earns billions of dollars in income through the operation of the Suez Canal.

In the 1950s, Nasser nationalized many of Egypt's resources, putting them under the control of the Egyptian government. Today, Egypt's nationalized resources and industries include the Suez Canal, the Aswan High Dam, and two major banks. In addition, the Egyptian government subsidizes, or helps pay for, some goods and services for its citizens. This is common in a socialist economy. The most famous subsidized good in Egypt is bread. Egyptians can purchase bread for less money than it costs to produce, with the government making up the difference in price. In capitalist economies, people own basic goods and services privately and have a lot of freedom to start their own businesses. This is broadly true in Egypt as well. The country has a large private sector, and it participates in the larger global capitalist economy. For example, one of the country's most famous billionaires is Naguib Sawiris. He owns Orascom, a giant private construction company that has branches in communications, mining, and other industries.

In addition, the Egyptian military is a large part of Egypt's economy. The military makes a great deal of money by doing development and construction projects for the Egyptian government. When governments take on projects like building schools or roads, they typically hire contractors, companies that agree to do the job for a set amount of money. The Egyptian military is the contractor for many of the Egyptian government's largest and most expensive projects. For example, in 2020 the Egyptian government was in the middle of a large development project in the Sinai Peninsula. Of the 600 billion Egyptian pounds (about $38 billion in US dollars) it spent on these projects, half of the money went to military organizations.[4]

Egypt's financial sector combines two different styles of banking. Most international banks, including some in Egypt, operate by investing their clients' money and returning it with interest, as well as giving loans such as mortgages. They earn money by charging interest on loans. However, the Islamic faith prohibits the charging of interest on loans. Instead, Islamic banks make money by requiring their clients to share profits from investments. The largest and most powerful banks in

Egypt work according to the international style. However, in 2022, there were 14 licensed Islamic banks in Egypt, and several major banks offered Islamic banking options.[5]

AGRICULTURE

About one-quarter of Egyptians make their living in agriculture. The most popular crop grown in Egypt is sugarcane, and it is also among Egypt's biggest agricultural exports. Other major crops include wheat, oranges, and onions.

Egypt is also famous for its cotton production. Egyptian cotton has a reputation for high quality. The cotton plant, after flowering, produces fluffy white fibers that can be picked, spun, and turned into inexpensive cloth. The Nile Delta region has grown cotton for about 7,000 years.

Egypt grows extra-long-staple, or Pima, cotton. This type of cotton is very soft and rare. Just 3 percent of cotton grown in the world is Pima.[6] Today, most cotton is harvested by machines. However, cotton in Egypt is picked by hand. This can help preserve the delicate fibers of the plant. Both the type of cotton and the picking method are

FISHING IN EGYPT

The fishing industry in Egypt operates in the Mediterranean Sea, in the Nile, and on lakes. Most of the fish caught in Egypt are farmed, meaning they come from fisheries rather than from the wild. The Egyptian fishing industry has grown quickly since the 2010s, increasing almost 18 percent between 2016 and 2020.[7] The government's plan to use four Egyptian lakes as fisheries helped spur the rise in production. Egypt is now the largest fish farmer in Africa.

Egypt's cotton industry requires significant manual labor.

why Egypt is famous for its cotton. But picking cotton is difficult work involving hours of manual labor in hot, sunny fields. It is often done by child laborers.

The cotton industry is also an example of some trends in Egypt's economic history. In the late 1800s, Egypt made the majority of its earnings from cotton. In the 1960s, Nasser nationalized the cotton industry, bringing it under government control. The cotton business became private again in 1994. This meant that Egyptian citizens could start their own cotton farms and businesses. However, today the Egyptian government oversees which types of cotton seeds are grown in the country. The political instability of the 2010s led to decreases in cotton quality and production. Egypt's exports dropped, and the reputation of its cotton was damaged. Egyptian cotton producers are now working to sell more high-quality cotton abroad.

IMPORTS, EXPORTS, AND MANUFACTURING

Exports are goods that a country or business sells to another country. Imports are goods that are bought from another country. The balance of trade is the value of a country's exports minus the value of

EVER GIVEN

The *Ever Given* is a container ship designed to transport goods across the ocean. It was built in 2018 and sails under the flag of Panama. It's one of the largest container ships in the world. In 2021, the *Ever Given* was traveling through the Suez Canal when it became stuck, blocking the canal for six days. During that time, no other ship could pass through the canal, and experts estimated that the accident caused a daily loss of $10 billion in trade.[8] Afterward, the Egyptian government promised to improve its protocols to avoid future accidents.

its imports. Egypt has a negative trade balance, which means that it imports more goods than it exports. Egypt's biggest imports are oil, wheat, cars, and medicines. Its biggest exports are oil, gold, natural gas, and fertilizers. The reason Egypt both imports and exports oil is because it needs more oil than the country can produce, but it can also make money from trading some of its own supply. Natural gas is another one of Egypt's biggest natural resources. Natural gas forms when fossils deep underground are heated and compressed over time. The resulting gas can be used as fuel. Egypt has the sixteenth-largest store of natural gas in the world.[9] It exports the gas via a system called the Arab gas pipeline, which runs across the Sinai Peninsula into Western Asia.

Manufacturing is the creation of new goods on a large scale at facilities such as factories. Egypt is growing its pharmaceutical manufacturing industry. The country is known

Offshore platforms in the Gulf of Suez extract underground oil and natural gas.

for its production of affordable drugs for common illnesses such as hepatitis C. The pharmaceutical industry is growing in part due to heavy investment from the Egyptian government. While the industry is not nationalized, the Egyptian government decided to create what it called a pharmaceutical city in order to increase the industry's growth. This project is part of a larger Egyptian government plan called Egypt Vision 2030. The "Vision" in the name is one of large-scale development of business and education.

In April 2021, President el-Sisi announced the opening of the pharmaceutical city. Called Gypto Pharma City, the 45-acre (18 ha) compound of buildings is located in a suburb of Cairo. Gypto Pharma City includes research buildings as well as factories for producing medicines. It is capable of producing 150 drugs, and there are plans to develop treatments for illnesses such as cancer in the future. According to a 2022 report, exports of pharmaceuticals increased in Egypt since the construction of the Pharma City. The pharmaceutical industry, like many others in Egypt, also has military connections. In 2017, the Egyptian military launched its own pharmaceutical company.

FOREIGN INVESTMENT

Egypt's natural resources and large workforce make it an attractive place for international companies to do business. Many East Asian companies have sought to invest in Egypt's economic growth. For example, a Chinese construction company has invested heavily in a widespread Egyptian construction project that will include Africa's new tallest building. And in 2022, the Japanese auto parts company Yazaki announced that it would invest in a new Egyptian factory.

Workers at Gypto Pharma City conduct advanced pharmaceutical research.

THE EGYPTIAN TOURISM INDUSTRY

Egypt's tourism industry is thousands of years old. Historical documents, as well as tomb graffiti, show that the ancient Greeks and Romans used to visit Egypt to see its pyramids and ruins. After the discovery of the Rosetta Stone in 1799, many Europeans became fascinated by Egypt. As transportation technology improved in the 1800s, the country became a popular tourist destination for Europeans. The tourism industry is very important to the Egyptian economy.

Egyptian tour guides show visitors through the nation's wealth of historic temples and ruins. In 2018, the tourism industry brought in more than $9 billion.

Although the tourism economy includes the sale of goods such as souvenirs, it is mainly a service-based economy. People sell the experiences associated with a visit to Egypt, such as hotel stays, transport, and guided tours. Almost 10 percent of Egyptians work in tourism. They engage in a wide variety of jobs, including housekeepers for tourist hotels, scuba instructors, Nile cruise ship drivers, museum tour guides, and much more.

Egypt's ancient ruins, religious destinations, and coastline help ensure that people will always want to visit. However, the tourism industry is susceptible to changes in Egypt's political climate. When Egypt is politically unstable, tourists are less likely to plan trips. Global factors like the strength of the world's economy or the presence of a pandemic also greatly affect tourism. When the COVID-19 pandemic began in early 2020, it led to global lockdowns and pauses on travel. Egypt's tourism business suffered. The country saw a 70 percent loss in tourism business in that year.[10] In July 2020, Egypt began allowing international visitors back into the country with proof of a negative COVID test. By late 2021, Egypt's tourism industry was making a strong recovery.

CHAPTER **EIGHT**

EGYPT TODAY

Egyptian culture is vibrant, social, and energetic. Egyptians enjoy gathering together whenever possible, and it's often considered strange to eat alone. The average number of children in an Egyptian family is three, and large families are common.[1] In general, Egyptians tend to dress more modestly than people in Western countries. Both men and women cover their bodies, and it's common for Muslim women to wear a hijab. In Egypt, men and women do not typically show physical affection in public. However, it's common in friendships between men to show closeness with gestures such as holding hands.

Because Islam's holy day is Friday, the Egyptian weekend is on Friday and Saturday, not on Saturday

Muslim prayer practices are an important part of Egypt's culture, and many Egyptians pray together on Fridays.

and Sunday. On Fridays, businesses close so that people can attend noon prayer at a mosque. Egyptian Muslims celebrate the traditional Islamic holidays of Eid al-Adha and Eid al-Fitr. They also celebrate the unofficial holidays of Mawlid al-Nabi, which recognizes the Prophet Muhammad's birthday, and Laylat al-Mi'raj, which commemorates the night the Prophet is said to have gone to Paradise. Coptic Christians celebrate Christian holidays, such as Christmas and Easter, according to their calendar. Egypt's national holidays include two separate Revolution Days—one commemorating the 1952 fall of the monarchy, and the other the 2013 uprising—and Armed Forces Day. There are also Egyptian holidays with their roots in ancient Egyptian traditions. For example, in June people celebrate the Nile's waters beginning to rise. On this holiday, people picnic along the Nile's banks and try to read their fortunes on balls of bread dough left out overnight.

Egyptian cities have a rich and active nightlife. It usually revolves more around shopping, conversation, and outdoor meals than bars or clubs. Stores and cafés are often open very late so people can shop and socialize in the cooler night temperatures.

According to a 2018 Pew survey, 62 percent of Egyptians attend religious services weekly.[3]

EGYPTIAN KIDS AND TEENS

One-third of Egyptians are younger than 15, representing a large and powerful new generation.[2] Egyptian kids and teens must attend school from

For students in Egypt, a field trip to ancient historic sites is often just a short bus ride away.

ages six to 15. Due to both underfunding and population growth, Egypt's schools tend to be very crowded. Some classes in the country fit as many as 70 students into one room.[4]

In general, young Egyptians tend to be more technologically knowledgeable than previous generations, and they are more likely to seek out information online. The interests and activities of Egyptian kids and teens vary widely from place to place. Just as Egyptian adults may live in crowded cities, beachside towns, or nomadic groups, Egyptian kids and teens have a diverse range of lifestyles. Some kids and teens train to take on family businesses at an early age, while others focus on preparing for the test that determines whether they find a spot at Egypt's public colleges. For many Egyptian kids and teens, the COVID-19 lockdown of 2020 was a very challenging time. Egyptian children who play sports tend to do so at clubs, and the pandemic reduced opportunities to gather at these facilities. During the pandemic, access to hobbies and time spent seeing friends dropped sharply. Many Egyptian kids experienced mental health issues, such as increased anxiety, as COVID-19 spread around their country and the world.

> **COVID-19 IN EGYPT**
>
> The first confirmed case of COVID-19 in Egypt was discovered on February 14, 2020. In March 2020, the Egyptian government implemented a lockdown. But by April, when Ramadan took place, the government had loosened restrictions such as curfews and restaurant closures. At the peak of the pandemic in Egypt, in February 2022, cases averaged more than 2,300 per day.[5] By April 2022, 43 percent of Egyptians had received at least one dose of a COVID-19 vaccine.[6]

Like students in other countries, university students in Egypt wore masks and practiced physical distancing during the COVID-19 pandemic.

EGYPT'S ONGOING STRUGGLES

Although Egyptians are united by the land and culture they share, the country struggles with inequality and discrimination. Poverty is a major issue in the country, as is homelessness. According to 2019 information from Egypt's Ministry of Social Solidarity, 12 million Egyptians, or more than one-tenth of the population, either have no home or live in a slum. Children make up

A police officer on an anti-sexual harassment force patrols the streets of Cairo.

one-quarter of Egypt's population experiencing homelessness.[7] These children are especially vulnerable to violence and health risks. The COVID-19 pandemic was especially hard on Egypt's children and teens experiencing homelessness, as they often depend on begging or selling small items to make ends meet.

Egyptian society also has high levels of gender inequality. Women in Egyptian society are about three times less likely to work outside the home than men are. Child marriage is common, with a little over 10 percent of Egyptian girls marrying before the legal age of 18.[8] Girls who marry before age 18 are more likely to drop out of school, experience intimate partner violence, and give birth to children who die young. Intimate partner violence is common in the country. A 2018 survey found that about 15 percent of women and girls reported abuse by a partner in the previous year.[9]

One of Egypt's most pressing gender equality issues is the problem of sexual and street harassment in the country. It's common for women and girls to experience catcalls, unwanted touching, or sexual attacks while out in public. A Reuters study of 19 large global cities found that Cairo ranked last in terms of women's safety.[10] In 2020, the case of a young man named Ahmed Bassam Zaki, called ABZ in the press, helped reignite the Egyptian conversation around street harassment. Zaki was a 21-year-old student when he was accused of sexual misconduct by more than 50 women and girls. He later received an eight-year prison sentence for sexual assault.[11] As Zeina Amr, an activist who founded the social media page Catcalls of Cairo, explained, after the case, "Suddenly everyone was talking about sexual harassment in Egypt in an overwhelming way."[12] The case has been described as a key moment in Egypt's #MeToo movement.

Discrimination against LGBTQ people, Egypt's Coptic Christian minority, and migrants also divide Egyptian society. Some Egyptians and immigrants face racism in the form of slurs, bullying, and violence. The Egyptian concept of race is not like the American one. Most Egyptians identify as Egyptian, not as a race. In addition, "Egyptian" is

LGBTQ PEOPLE IN EGYPT

It is not illegal to be gay, lesbian, bisexual, or transgender in Egypt. However, LGBTQ Egyptians experience discrimination. Sometimes LGBTQ people are arrested for debauchery, a vague term for inappropriate sexual behavior. According to a 2020 Human Rights Watch report, Egyptian police and security officers target LGBTQ people for arrests, detention, and torture. Some people interviewed for the report said they were arrested after showing public support for LGBTQ rights.

usually considered an Arab identity, one whose main feature is speaking the Arabic language and participating in Arab traditions. "Arab" is also not a racial identity in the American sense of the word. Native Arabic speakers come from many races. Nevertheless, there is a trend in Egyptian society of discrimination against people with darker skin or who are of non-Egyptian African origin. Nubians, who are often identified as Black, face negative stereotypes and underrepresentation in Egyptian society. However, there are many Egyptians working to make their society fairer and more inclusive for everyone who lives there. Activists like Zeina Amr are giving a voice to critics of street harassment. Nubian and Sudanese activists risk arrest and police violence in order to advocate for the rights of marginalized Egyptians.

EGYPT LOOKS TO THE FUTURE

Egypt's population is growing, and young Egyptians will need more space. Since 2015, the Egyptian government has been building a new capital city called New Cairo. The city is a $58 billion project largely carried out by military contractors.[13] When it is done, it will be 28 miles (45 km) east of Cairo, covering an area the size of Singapore.[14] The goal

IMMIGRATION TO EGYPT

Many immigrants to Egypt are from other Arabic-speaking countries. In 2021, the largest group of migrants to Egypt were from Palestine. The second-largest group of migrants came from Syria, another Arabic-speaking country in the same region. It can be difficult for immigrants to Egypt to settle permanently in the country. A 2018 law states that foreigners who wish to apply for Egyptian citizenship must pay seven million pounds, equivalent to about $400,000 at the time.[15]

The planned capital city of New Cairo features buildings arranged in neatly planned grids and curves.

of the project is to relieve Cairo's congestion, attract businesses, and house the next generation of Egyptians. In the meantime, scientists, activists, and nonprofits are working to prevent the negative impacts of climate change so that Egypt can continue to benefit from its river, seas,

and wildlife. For example, a German-Egyptian forest planting project is attempting to cultivate more wooded areas in the country. Its goal is to use sewage water to grow trees that can provide food and income for Egyptians while also helping to remove carbon from the atmosphere.

More than a decade after the Arab Spring, the nation's young people still use social media and street protests to make their voices heard, even in the face of serious danger. Egypt's next generation of leaders faces a challenging political and social landscape. But many believe that they can hold on to their country's rich and ancient history while paving the way for a brighter future.

Egypt has faced significant turmoil in the first few decades of the 2000s, but today the nation's people are working hard toward a safer, more stable future.

ESSENTIAL FACTS

OFFICIAL NAME: THE ARAB REPUBLIC OF EGYPT

GEOGRAPHY

Area: 386,662 square miles (1,001,450 sq km)

Highest Elevation: Mount Katrina at 8,625 feet (2,629 m)

Lowest Elevation: The Qattara Depression at −436 feet (−133 m)

PEOPLE

Population: 107.8 million (2022 est.)

Most Populous City: Cairo (21.75 million)

Ethnic Groups: Egyptian

Religions: Islam, Christianity

GOVERNMENT

Type of Government: Presidential republic

Capital: Cairo

Head of State: President

Head of Government: Prime minister

Legislature: Bicameral, with a House of Representatives and a Senate

ECONOMY

Currency: Egyptian pound

Major Industries: Agriculture, textiles, tourism, pharmaceuticals

Natural Resources: Oil, natural gas, iron ore, limestone

NATIONAL SYMBOLS

National Anthem: "Bilady, Bilady, Bilady" ("My Homeland, My Homeland, My Homeland")

National Bird: Steppe eagle

National Flower: Blue lotus

GLOSSARY

BICAMERAL
Having two legislative chambers.

CONCENTRATION CAMP
A place where prisoners of war, political prisoners, or refugees are held in poor conditions and are forced to work.

DELTA
The place where a river empties into a sea.

DOMESTICATED
Adapted to live among or be of use to people.

MARTIAL LAW
The replacement of civilian rule with military control.

NATIONALIZE
To bring under the control of a country's government.

NOMADIC
Moving from one place to another.

PHARAOH
An ancient Egyptian ruler who was considered a god.

PHARMACEUTICAL
Relating to medicines.

POACHING
The illegal taking of wild animals.

SILT
Fine sediment, made up of sand, clay, or other material, that is deposited by flowing water.

SOUND STAGE
A place where movies and television shows are filmed.

STREET HARASSMENT
Unwanted speech or touching directed at strangers in public.

VICEROY
A local ruler who uses power on behalf of a higher central authority.

WADI
A temporary stream of water that dries up and then reappears.

ADDITIONAL RESOURCES

SELECTED BIBLIOGRAPHY

"Egypt." *World Factbook*, 2022, cia.gov. Accessed 22 Apr. 2022.

Goldschmidt, Arthur Eduard. "Egypt." *Encyclopedia Britannica*, 2 Nov. 2021, britannica.com. Accessed 22 Apr. 2022.

Mertz, Barbara. *Temples, Tombs, and Hieroglyphs: A Popular History of Ancient Egypt*. William Morrow, 2007.

FURTHER READINGS

Hart, George. *Ancient Egypt*. DK, 2021.

Honovich, Nancy. *1,000 Facts about Ancient Egypt*. National Geographic, 2019.

Nardo, Don. *Cause & Effect: Ancient Egypt*. ReferencePoint, 2018.

ONLINE RESOURCES

To learn more about Egypt, please visit **abdobooklinks.com** or scan this QR code. These links are routinely monitored and updated to provide the most current information available.

MORE INFORMATION

For more information on this subject, contact or visit the following organizations:

The Egyptian Museum
Tahrir Square, Downtown, Cairo - Egypt
egyptianmuseumcairo.com/egyptian-museum-cairo/
The Egyptian Museum in Cairo is among the largest and oldest archaeological museums in the Middle East.

Embassy of the Arab Republic of Egypt
3521 International Ct., NW
Washington, DC 20008
egyptembassy.net
The Embassy of Egypt represents the people and government of Egypt in the United States.

Nature Conservation Egypt
natureegypt.org
info@natureegypt.org
Nature Conservation Egypt leads science-based environmental and wildlife conservation projects inside Egypt.

SOURCE NOTES

CHAPTER 1. A TOUR OF EGYPT
1. Mostafa El-Abbadi. "Library of Alexandria." *Encyclopedia Britannica*, 17 July 2020, britannica.com. Accessed 21 June 2022.
2. "Egypt." *CIA World Factbook*, 15 June 2022, cia.gov. Accessed 21 June 2022.
3. "Pyramids of Giza." *Encyclopedia Britannica*, 1 Apr. 2022, britannica.com. Accessed 21 June 2022.
4. "Pyramids of Giza."
5. Barbara G. Mertz. "Memphis." *Encyclopedia Britannica*, 3 Dec. 2020, britannica.com. Accessed 21 June 2022.
6. "Saint Catherine's Monastery." *Encyclopedia Britannica*, 26 July 2021, britannica.com. Accessed 21 June 2022.
7. "African Countries by Population (2022)." *Worldometer*, 2022, worldometers.info. Accessed 21 June 2022.
8. "Arab Countries 2022." *World Population Review*, 2022, worldpopulationreview.com. Accessed 21 June 2022.

CHAPTER 2. GEOGRAPHY
1. "Egypt." *CIA World Factbook*, 15 June 2022, cia.gov. Accessed 21 June 2022.
2. "Egypt," *CIA World Factbook*.
3. "Egypt," *CIA World Factbook*.
4. "Nile River." *National Geographic*, n.d., education.nationalgeographic.org. Accessed 21 June 2022.
5. Jeffrey Allman Gritzner. "Sahara." *Encyclopedia Britannica*, 26 Nov. 2019, britannica.com. Accessed 21 June 2022.
6. "Ocean Shipping and Shipbuilding." *OECD*, n.d., oecd.org. Accessed 21 June 2022.
7. "Main Four Egypt Ports." *Egypt Tours Portal*, 29 Sept. 2021, egypttoursportal.com. Accessed 21 June 2022.
8. "Monthly Weather Forecast and Climate." *Weather Atlas*, n.d., weather-atlas.com. Accessed 21 June 2022.

CHAPTER 3. PLANTS AND ANIMALS
1. Frans Witte, et al. "Fish Fauna of the Nile." *ResearchGate*, January 2009, researchgate.net. Accessed 21 June 2022.
2. Waleed Hamza. "The Nile Fishes and Fisheries." *IntechOpen*, 14 May 2014, intechopen.com. Accessed 21 June 2022.
3. "Marbled Lungfish." *Fishbase*, n.d., fishbase.de. Accessed 21 June 2022.
4. "Cobra." *Encyclopedia Britannica*, 26 Apr. 2017, britannica.com. Accessed 21 June 2022.
5. "Forest Area (% of Land Area) – Egypt, Arab Rep." *World Bank*, n.d., data.worldbank.org. Accessed 21 June 2022.
6. "Egypt Moves to Protect 45 Rare Endemic Plant Species from Climate Change Impact." *Egypt Today*, 2 Apr. 2022, egypttoday.com. Accessed 21 June 2022.

CHAPTER 4. HISTORY

1. John Slight. "After the First World War: The 1919 Egyptian Revolution." *The Open University*, 18 Jan. 2019, open.edu. Accessed 21 June 2022.
2. Raymond H. Anderson. "Nasser Funeral Is Disrupted by Frenzy of Millions." *New York Times*, 2 Oct. 1970, nytimes.com. Accessed 21 June 2022.
3. "Anwar Sadat." *Encyclopedia Britannica*, 21 Dec. 2021, britannica.com. Accessed 21 June 2022.
4. "Suez Canal Revenues Hit $6.3 Bln in 2021 vs $5.6 Bln in 2020." *Reuters*, 2 Jan. 2022, reuters.com. Accessed 21 June 2022.

CHAPTER 5. PEOPLE AND CULTURE

1. "Egypt." *CIA World Factbook*, 15 June 2022, cia.gov. Accessed 21 June 2022.
2. "2020 Report on International Religious Freedom: Egypt." *US Department of State*, 12 May 2021, state.gov. Accessed 21 June 2022.
3. David D. Kirkpatrick. "A Timeline of Jews in Egypt." *New York Times*, 23 June 2015, nytimes.com. Accessed 21 June 2022.
4. Kirkpatrick, "A Timeline of Jews in Egypt."
5. "Egypt." *World Jewish Congress*, n.d., worldjewishcongress.org. Accessed 21 June 2022.
6. "Egypt," *CIA World Factbook*.
7. "Egypt," *CIA World Factbook*.
8. "Population, Total – Egypt, Arab Rep." *World Bank*, n.d., data.worldbank.org. Accessed 21 June 2022.
9. "Hollywood of the Middle East." *Pilot*, n.d., nabpilot.org. Accessed 21 June 2022.
10. Denys Johnson-Davies. "Naguib Mahfouz." *Guardian*, 30 Aug. 2006, theguardian.com. Accessed 21 June 2022.
11. "Homage to Egypt's 'Fourth Pyramid.'" *Qantara*, 1 Sept. 2008, en.qantara.de. Accessed 21 June 2022.
12. "Egypt." *FIFA*, 2022, fifa.com. Accessed 21 June 2022.
13. "Egypt Premier League." *Soccerway*, 2022, us.soccerway.com. Accessed 21 June 2022.
14. "Borg El Arab Stadium." *Sportsmatik*, 19 Feb. 2021, sportsmatik.com. Accessed 21 June 2022.
15. Michael LoRé. "Why Egyptians Are So Dominant at Squash." *Culture Trip*, 9 Feb. 2018, theculturetrip.com. Accessed 21 June 2022.
16. "How Tobacco Use in Egypt Affects Poverty and COVID-19 Cases." *Borgen Magazine*, 11 Sept. 2020, borgenmagazine.com. Accessed 21 June 2022.
17. "Alexandria, Egypt Metro Area Population 1950–2022." *Macrotrends*, n.d., macrotrends.net. Accessed 21 June 2022.
18. "Egypt," *CIA World Factbook*.
19. Hafez Ghanem. "Improving Regional and Rural Development for Inclusive Growth in Egypt." *Brookings Institution*, Jan. 2014, brookings.edu. Accessed 21 June 2022.

SOURCE NOTES CONTINUED

CHAPTER 6. POLITICS
1. "Abdel Fattah al-Sisi." *Encyclopedia Britannica*, 15 Nov. 2021, britannica.com. Accessed 21 June 2022.
2. "Egypt's 2018 Presidential 'Election': What You Need to Know." *Al Jazeera*, 16 Mar. 2018, aljazeera.com. Accessed 21 June 2022.
3. "'Biggest Crackdown' under Sisi Condemned after Thousands Arrested." *Al Jazeera*, 2 Oct. 2019, aljazeera.com. Accessed 21 June 2022.
4. "Egypt Election: Sisi Secures Landslide Win." *BBC News*, 29 May 2014, bbc.com. Accessed 21 June 2022.
5. "Egypt." *CIA World Factbook*, 15 June 2022, cia.gov. Accessed 21 June 2022.
6. Jacob Wirtschafter and Mina Nader. "Ahead of el-Sisi Election, Youths Feel Like Egypt Has Lost Its Way." *USA Today*, 23 Mar. 2018, usatoday.com. Accessed 21 June 2022.
7. Wirtschafter and Nader, "Ahead of el-Sisi Election."

CHAPTER 7. ECONOMICS
1. "Egypt." *CIA World Factbook*, 15 June 2022, cia.gov. Accessed 21 June 2022.
2. "Convert Egyptian Pounds to US Dollars." *XE*, n.d., xe.com. Accessed 21 June 2022.
3. "GDP (Current US$) – Egypt, Arab Rep." *World Bank*, n.d., data.worldbank.org. Accessed 21 June 2022.
4. Yezid Sayigh. "Egypt's Military as the Spearhead of State Capitalism." *Carnegie Middle East Center*, 26 Oct. 2020, carnegie-mec.org. Accessed 21 June 2022.
5. Hossam Mounir. "Islamic Banking in Egypt Amounts to EGP 429bn in 2021: Eifa." *Daily News Egypt*, 5 Mar. 2022, dailynewsegypt.com. Accessed 21 June 2022.
6. Yasmine Al-Sayyad. "The End of Egyptian Cotton." *New Yorker*, 27 Feb. 2020, newyorker.com. Accessed 21 June 2022.
7. Ahmed Wally and Olutayo O. Akingbe. "An Overview of the Aquaculture Industry in Egypt." *USDA*, 15 Feb. 2022, apps.fas.usda.gov. Accessed 21 June 2022.
8. Vivian Yee and James Glanz. "How One of the World's Biggest Ships Jammed the Suez Canal." *New York Times*, 19 July 2021, nytimes.com. Accessed 21 June 2022.
9. "Egypt Natural Gas." *Worldometer*, n.d., worldometers.info. Accessed 21 June 2022.
10. Mohamed Saied. "Egypt Hopes Israeli Tourists Will Make Up Losses from Ukraine War." *Al-Monitor*, 12 Apr. 2022, al-monitor.com. Accessed 21 June 2022.

CHAPTER 8. EGYPT TODAY
   1. "Egypt." *CIA World Factbook*, 15 June 2022, cia.gov. Accessed 21 June 2022.
   2. "Egypt Back to School: New School Year Begins with Overcrowded Classes." *YouTube*, uploaded by TRT World, 4 Oct. 2018, youtube.com. Accessed 21 June 2022.
   3. "How Religious Commitment Varies by Country among People of All Ages." *Pew Research Center*, 13 June 2018, pewresearch.org. Accessed 21 June 2022.
   4. "Egypt Back to School."
   5. "Egypt: Coronavirus Pandemic Country Profile." *Our World in Data*, 21 June 2022, ourworldindata.org. Accessed 21 June 2022.
   6. "Coronavirus (COVID-19) Vaccinations." *Our World in Data*, 21 June 2022, ourworldindata.org. Accessed 21 June 2022.
   7. Reem Leila. "Fighting Homelessness in Egypt: 'We Are with You.'" *Ahram Online*, 25 Jan. 2019, english.ahram.org.eg. Accessed 21 June 2022.
   8. "Policy for Action: Ending Child Marriage." *UNICEF*, n.d., unicef.org. Accessed 21 June 2022.
   9. "Egypt." *UN Women*, n.d., data.unwomen.org. Accessed 21 June 2022.
   10. Laila Mohammed. "Sexual Harassment in Egypt: A Crisis Searching for a Cure." *Arab News*, 4 July 2020, arabnews.com. Accessed 21 June 2022.
   11. Olivia Mustafa. "Ahmad Bassam Zaki Sentenced to 8 Years in Prison for Sexual Assault." *Egyptian Streets*, 11 Apr. 2021, egyptianstreets.com. Accessed 21 June 2022.
   12. "Zeina Amr—Catcalls of Cairo and Egypt's Movement against Sexual Harassment." *Egyptian Streets Podcast*, 15 Aug. 2021, anchor.fm. Accessed 21 June 2022.
   13. Aidan Lewis and Mohamed Abdellah. "Egypt's New Desert Capital Faces Delays as It Battles for Funds." *Reuters*, 13 May 2019, reuters.com. Accessed 21 June 2022.
   14. Mustafa Menshawy. "Why Is Egypt Building a New Capital?" *Al Jazeera*, 5 July 2021, aljazeera.com. Accessed 21 June 2022.
   15. "Egypt: President Ratifies Law Amending Residency and Citizenship Laws." *Library of Congress*, 27 Aug. 2018, loc.gov. Accessed 21 June 2022.

INDEX

agriculture, 63, 80–82
al-Aswany, Alaa, 56–57
alcohol, 62
Alexandria, 4, 6, 17, 18–19, 21, 39, 40, 49, 59, 60, 63
ancient Egypt, 6, 9–10, 18, 26, 28, 36–40, 42, 57, 87, 90
Arab League, 72
Arab Spring, 66
Arabic, 6, 12, 42, 53, 54, 59, 63, 96
Aswan High Dam, 16–18, 47, 49, 78

Bedouins, 53, 63
Begin, Menachem, 48
birds, 28
blue lotus, 24

Cairo, 7, 9, 10, 17, 18, 42, 43, 50, 54, 56, 60, 63, 66, 84, 95, 97
camels, 7, 31, 52
children, 54, 67, 88, 92, 93–94
Christianity, 6, 11, 12, 40, 50, 57, 69, 72, 90, 95
Cleopatra, 38, 40

climate, 21–22
climate change, 12, 22, 32, 97
Coptic, 6, 54, 57, 72, 90, 95
coral reefs, 10, 21, 32, 34
cotton, 80–82
COVID-19 pandemic, 87, 92, 94
crocodiles, 28
currency, 74

dugongs, 10, 32

education, 54, 90–92, 94
Egyptian Armed Forces, 56, 66–67, 70, 72, 79, 84, 90
Egyptian Museum, 9
elections, 47, 64, 66–67, 68–71
el-Sisi, Abdel Fattah, 67, 72, 84
endangered species, 32
Ever Given, 82
exports, 80, 82–83, 84

families, 56, 88, 92
financial sector, 79–80
fishing, 18, 21, 26, 32, 36, 80
food, 9, 60–61

forests, 29, 98

gender inequality, 94–95
government structure, 68–69

Hatshepsut, 38
hieroglyphs, 9, 38, 39, 42
hijab, 6, 88

immigration, 52, 95–96
imports, 82–83
Islam, 6, 10, 40–42, 43, 50, 62, 64–66, 70, 79–80, 88–90
Israel, 14, 48, 52

Judaism, 12, 50, 52

koshari, 9, 61
Kulthūm, Umm, 58, 59

Lake Nasser, 17, 18, 26, 28
LGBTQ people, 95
Library of Alexandria, 6
Libya, 14, 16, 39, 40
literature, 56–57

Mahfouz, Naguib, 56
Mamluk Sultanate, 42–43
mammals, 29, 31
media, 54–56
Mediterranean Sea, 14–16, 17, 18–19, 21, 31, 40, 60, 80
Morsi, Mohamed, 66–67, 70
Mount Katrina, 14, 16, 17
Mubarak, Hosni, 12, 48, 64–66, 70
music, 57–59
Muslim Brotherhood, 66, 70

Nasser, Gamal Abdel, 44–47, 49, 52, 53, 68, 69, 78, 82
New Cairo, 96–97
Nile River, 7, 12, 16–19, 22, 24, 26, 28, 32, 38, 47, 63, 80, 87, 90
Nubia, 40, 54, 96

Ottoman Empire, 43

pan-Arabism, 69
papyrus, 9, 24–26
pharmaceutical industry, 83–84
political parties, 69–70

poverty, 66, 74, 93
prehistoric Egypt, 36–38
Pyramids of Giza, 7, 9, 17, 38

Ramadan, 54–56, 92
Red Sea, 10, 14, 17, 19, 21, 31–32, 34, 40
reptiles, 28, 29
Rosetta Stone, 42, 85

Sadat, Anwar, 47–48, 64
Sahara Desert, 7, 16, 19, 21, 22, 28–29, 63
Saint Catherine's Monastery, 11
Salah, Mohamed, 59, 60
scarab, 31
scorpion, 29
sexual harassment, 95
Sinai Peninsula, 10, 14, 21, 40, 48, 63, 71, 79, 83
Siwa Oasis, 17, 19
Six-Day War, 49
socialism, 44, 49, 76, 78–79
sports, 31, 59–60
succulents, 29

Sudan, 14, 16, 17, 40
Suez Canal, 14, 17, 21, 31, 46, 48, 49, 52, 78, 82

Tahrir Square, 66
terrorism, 71–72
tobacco, 62
tourism, 31, 34, 85–87

United Kingdom, 43–44, 49, 52, 60

World War I, 43
World War II, 44, 52, 70

ABOUT THE AUTHOR

A. W. BUCKEY

A. W. Buckey is a writer living in Brooklyn, New York.